PALM BEACH PANORAMA:

TURN-OF-THE-CENTURY PHOTOGRAPHS

BY E. W. HAZARD

From an exhibit at the Henry Morrison Flagler Museum
March 10 - July 31, 1996
Text by Sandra Barghini

Mr. and Mrs. E.W. Hazard

Photographs by Emerson W. Hazard were generously donated to

the Henry Morrison Flagler Museum by Ruth K. Imhoff, E. W. Hazard's granddaughter, in 1988 and 1991.

Special thanks also go to Raymond Smith, a scholar whose unpublished biographical essay was

valuable in the development of this publication.

Emerson W. Hazard (1854-1926) was a photographer of great innovation and invention. His career spanned several decades in New England where he worked as a photographer in Southington, Connecticut from 1885 until his death in 1926. Shortly after attending the Philadelphia Centennial Exposition, where Americans of all types were dazzled by the American innovations in technology and culture, Hazard began a photographic apprenticeship with Frank Wheeler. In 1885 he opened his own photo studio.

Always interested in the innovative, Hazard became known for his unusual photographs. He liked large views of the Connecticut terrain, and photographed the outdoors from the hilltops surrounding his town. He experimented with movement in photos, and high speed photography, which was becoming well-known in the works of Muybridge at that time. He developed a method to shoot photos in quick succession to document a local yacht race. He also produced multiple exposure photos, and photographs of animals in nature - a difficult task to accomplish. His photos often became the subject of articles in the local paper, *The Southington Phoenix*. Because the paper was not actually able to reproduce the photos in printed format at this time, it would advertise their availability at Hazard's photo studio. An interested reader could thus have a complete package of a dramatic event, with both story and photos.

It was natural that Hazard would have an affinity for the panorama format which allowed him to show the expansiveness of the terrain. He also liked to use hand-held cameras. Most professional equipment in his day was cumbersome, but for his innovative projects, hand-held cameras allowed him more freedom. In 1900, Kodak, which had burst on the scene with innovations in equipment for amateur photographers, introduced the Kodak Panoram No. 1 and Kodak Panoram No. 4. Hazard used the Kodak Panoram No. 4, which produced photo prints 3" x 12". These cameras were simple to use, and considered to be "automatic". The lens swept across the camera's 142 degree angle from one side to the other.

What brought Emerson Hazard to Palm Beach in 1905 is not known. He could have been documenting *the season* for a local paper, or for a client in Palm Beach. *The Meriden Journal* announced that Hazard was leaving for Florida on January 4, 1905 and returned on April 15. The paper kept track of his photographic work in Florida, announcing on March 6, that Hazard had taken a large number of photos.

Hazard had always had an interest in the outdoors. He was an avid bicyclist and hunter. His views of Palm Beach are far from being just images of Palm Beach society in *the season*. He also photographed those in the wilderness of the area - settlers who lived in the jungle areas and ran tourist attractions - like Alligator Joe, or the unnamed orange juice stand owners, along one of the trails. One can't help but feel Hazard's sense of whimsy while looking at his view of the intrepid bicyclist confronted with the mass of mangroves.

But perhaps, for the modern day viewer, Hazard's documentation of a lifestyle which has disappeared from Palm Beach is the most important thing he has to show us. His view of the commonplace enlightens us and allows us to see a life which is no longer common, nor even extant on Palm Beach Island. It is a view of both sides of the Gilded Age, and one we do not often get a chance to see.

FLAGLER AND THE HOTEL BOOM

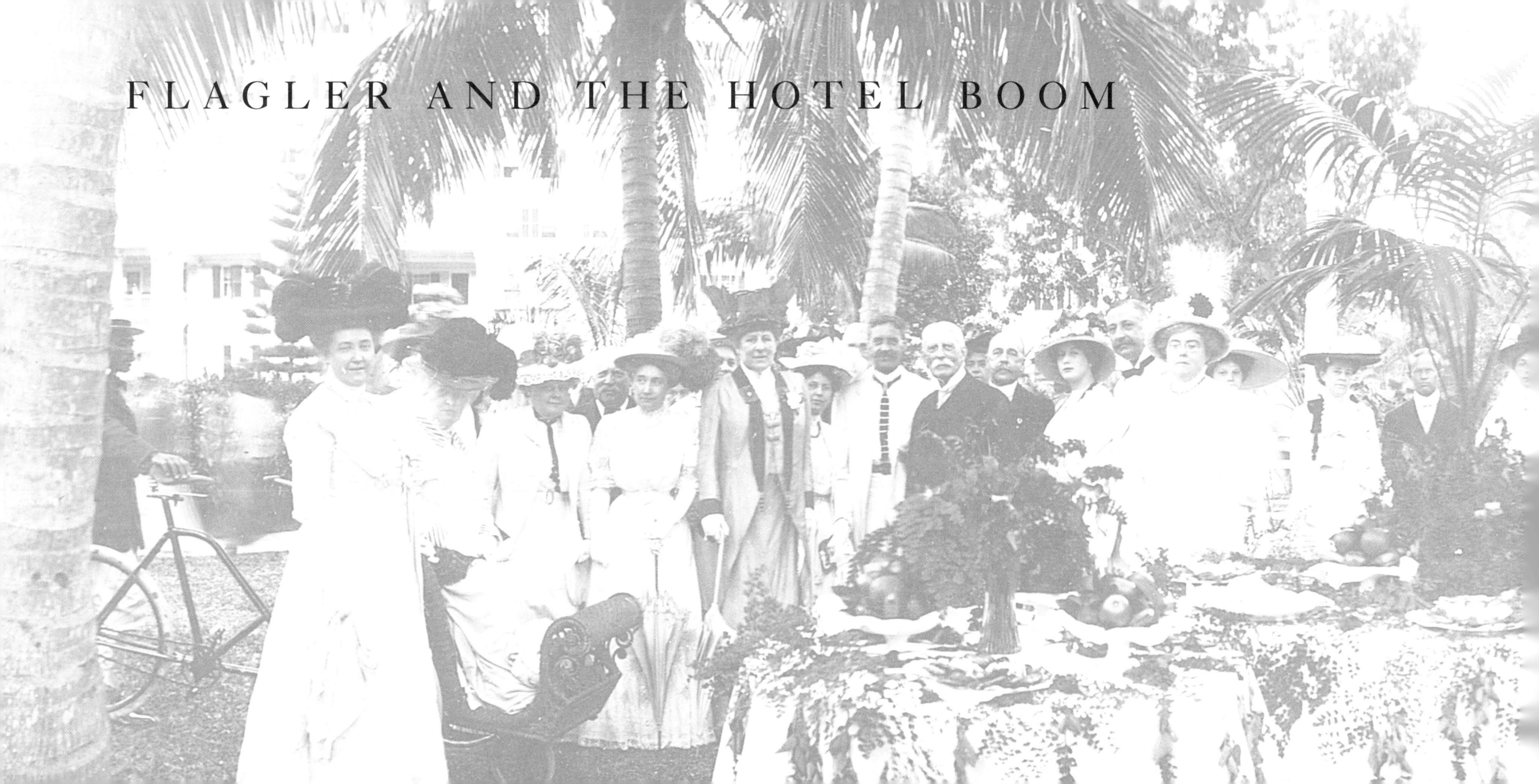

Palm Beach at the turn of the century was on the cusp of transforming itself into the modern, affluent and socially conscious town we know today. Henry Flagler had just completed one of the largest hotels in the world to service society clientele from places like Newport and New York, even building the train line to bring visitors to the town. For prominent families of the Gilded Age, Palm Beach was becoming *the* new place to winter, the most important people of the Eastern Seaboard had begun to enjoy the winter climate of Palm Beach for *the season*. But around 1905, this fancy and somewhat fanciful, Palm Beach was just a small incursion into the rest of the Island's wildness and frontier environment. Just beyond the luxury of the Royal Poinciana and The Breakers hotels a wild Florida thrived.

This period of change is the Palm Beach documented by E. W. Hazard in panorama photographs, while visiting Palm Beach beginning in the season of 1905. Through his creative and unusual photographs, the Connecticut photographer allows the contrast between the society Palm Beach and the frontier Palm Beach to surprise the modern viewer. No doubt, part of the charm of a visit to Palm Beach at the turn of the century was the fun of riding a bicycle down a trail overgrown with mangroves or visiting an alligator farm. But the juxtaposition of that part of life and Tea in the Cocoanut Grove is striking. Hazard gave both cultures a careful look. The Palm Beach which was being created as a winter resort when Hazard was taking photos, ca. 1905, has overtaken the natural wildness of the Island. Through his photographs we can see its beginning, and see a part of Palm Beach Island's history which no longer exists.

Whitehall was Henry Flagler's Palm Beach residence, opened for the first time for the season of 1902.

No. 3. HENRY M. FLAGLER'S WHITE HALL. LOOKING WEST FROM THE PONCIANA HOTEL ACROSS LAKE WORTH TO WEST PALM BEACH, FLA.

The Lake side of Palm Beach looking towards the commercial center of West Palm Beach. The railroad bridge and dock, and the popular travel agency "Ask Mr. Foster" are in view.

Along the Lake Trail, E.W. Hazard in front of the Beach Club.

TEA IN THE COCOANUT GROVE

Friends having Tea in the Cocoanut Grove. Henry Flagler in the center.

26 LOOKING EAST FROM TOP OF POINCIANA HOTEL SHOWING BREAKERS HOTEL AND OCEAN.

The Breakers hotel with a view of a cargo vessel sailing along the coast.

COCOA GROVE. TEA GARDEN ON THE PONCIANA GROUNDS PALM BEACH FLA.

The Cocoanut Grove was located between the Hotel Royal Poinciana and Whitehall, and was the daily meeting place for afternoon tea.

POINCIANA COLONADE.

Colonnaded porch at the Hotel Royal Poinciana.

No. 2   PONCIANA HOTEL

The Hotel Royal Poinciana, Flagler's first Palm Beach hotel, was a tribute to the modern age. It had elevators, private baths and electricity throughout.

The Palm Beach Hotel, a small hotel near the railroad depot, advertised room rates of $3.00 per day in 1900.

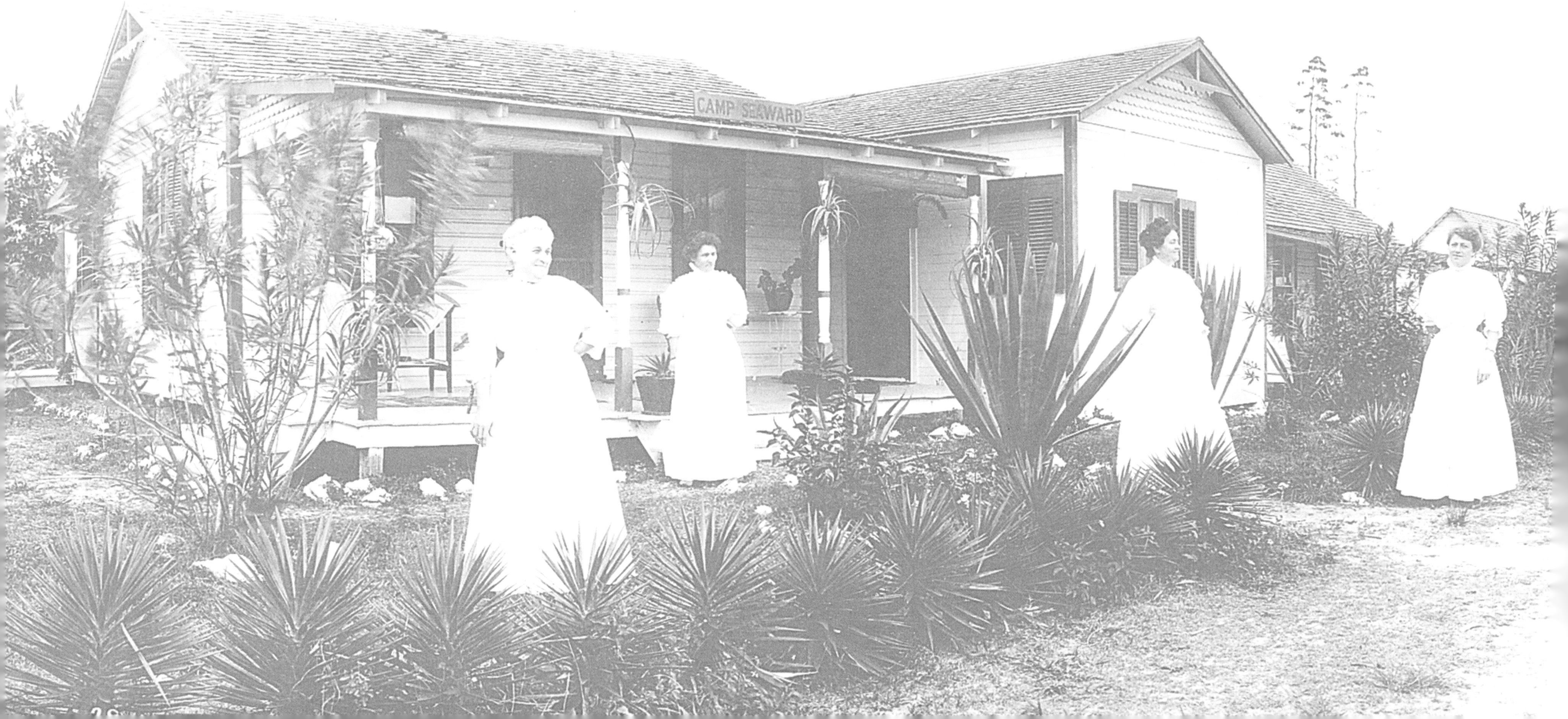
CAMP SEAWARD

SETTLERS AND WORKERS

Before the advent of the grand hotels, early rugged individualists had discovered wild Florida and built homes away from the hustle of northern cities they had left behind. Life on that Palm Beach was hard - residents built houses from lumber gathered on the beach from coastal shipwrecks, and sustenance came from wildlife which was hunted and fished - from possum to bear. When Flagler decided to build the grand hotels on the Island, workers were brought in and joined that earlier population, building homes along the trails or in areas designed for them. By 1905, life was no longer a struggle just to survive as it had been a short span of years earlier, but Hazard's photos still catch a glimpse of the wildness of earlier days of frontier life.

41 IN THE JUNGLE, FLA RESIDENCE OF ALLIGATOR JOE.

*In an ad from a 1900 newspaper Alligator Joe's Farm claimed "hundreds of crocodiles and alligators always in sight. Don't miss seeing Alligator Joe capture a gator single-handed."
Of course, Alligator souvenirs and Florida curios were on sale at the farm, and one could get a quick lunch of oysters and cold drinks.*

A LITTLE HOME ON LAKE WORTH FLA.

A prosperous settler's home on the Lake.

The Styx was the area populated by Black workers brought to Palm Beach mainly to build the Hotel Royal Poinciana. It was located in the vicinity of North County Road and Sunrise Avenue.

ROOTS TRAIL LOOKING WEST. P.B. FLA.

Roots Trail was located north of the hotels, not far from the Styx. No doubt these families were engaged in work at the large Island hotels.

THE STYX ON THE COUNTY ROAD P.B. FLA

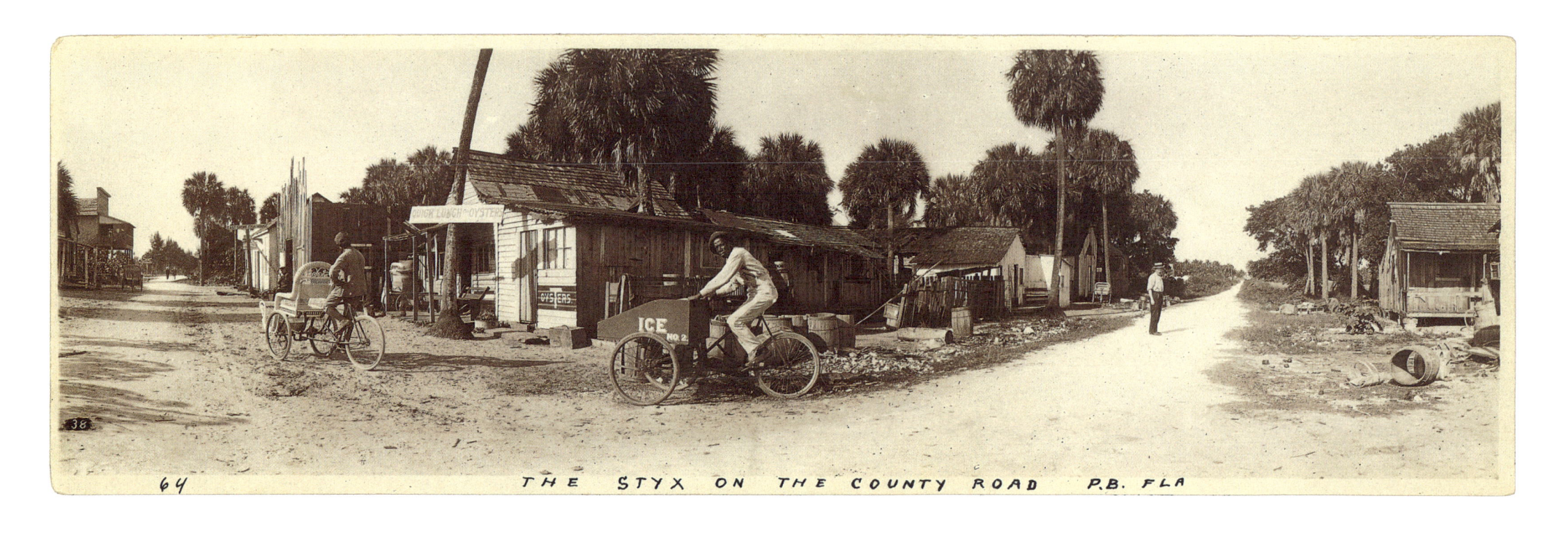

On the left, a man pedals an "Afromobile." These vehicles were used by visitors to Palm Beach to traverse the Island. Motorized vehicles were not allowed.

Fishing and hunting were the means of survival for early Palm Beach settlers. While civilization had arrived and changed the rugged character of life by 1905, there was still much open ocean front.

Pleasant times along the Roots Trail.

PASTIMES

While visitors to Palm Beach's luxury hotels could amuse themselves with many hotel activities, like Tea in the Cocoanut Grove, golf, or relaxing at the beach, some visitors were more adventurous. After the construction of the grand hotels, affluent winter visitors to Palm Beach explored the Island on trails which crossed between the hotels and the ocean, and along Lake Worth. A path cut through jungle vegetation where vacationers walked, bicycled or were pedaled in an "Afromobile," perhaps stopping to have a glass of iced orange juice. Off the Jungle Trail, the South Bound Trail led to Alligator Joe's alligator farm, a distinctive attraction for Northern visitors.

A visitor's choice - Alligator Joe's Farm or the Jungle Trail. The Jungle Trial was located where Worth Avenue is at present.

MANGROVE TREES. FLA JUNGLE.

An intrepid bicyclist stops to consider the Mangrove forest along the trail.

A respite from jungle activities - relaxing at the beach at The Breakers hotel.

A stop along the way for a cool drink.

This 1907 map of West Palm Beach and Palm Beach shows the major points of interest and roads. Produced just two years after Hazard photographed the Island, many of the places he photographed can be located on this map. On the north part of Palm Beach Island, The Breakers, Royal Poinciana and Palm Beach hotels can be seen, as well as Whitehall, the Cocoanut Grove and the railroad passenger depot. In the middle of the map Clark's trail and other trails traverse the Island from East to West, crossed by the North to South Jungle Trail and the County Road. Roots Trail does not appear on this map, as it was just north of the edge of it. Visitors to Palm Beach Island crossed over Lake Worth via the Railroad Bridge from West Palm Beach or by ferry. The ferry landings are visible on both sides of Lake Worth in the center of the map.

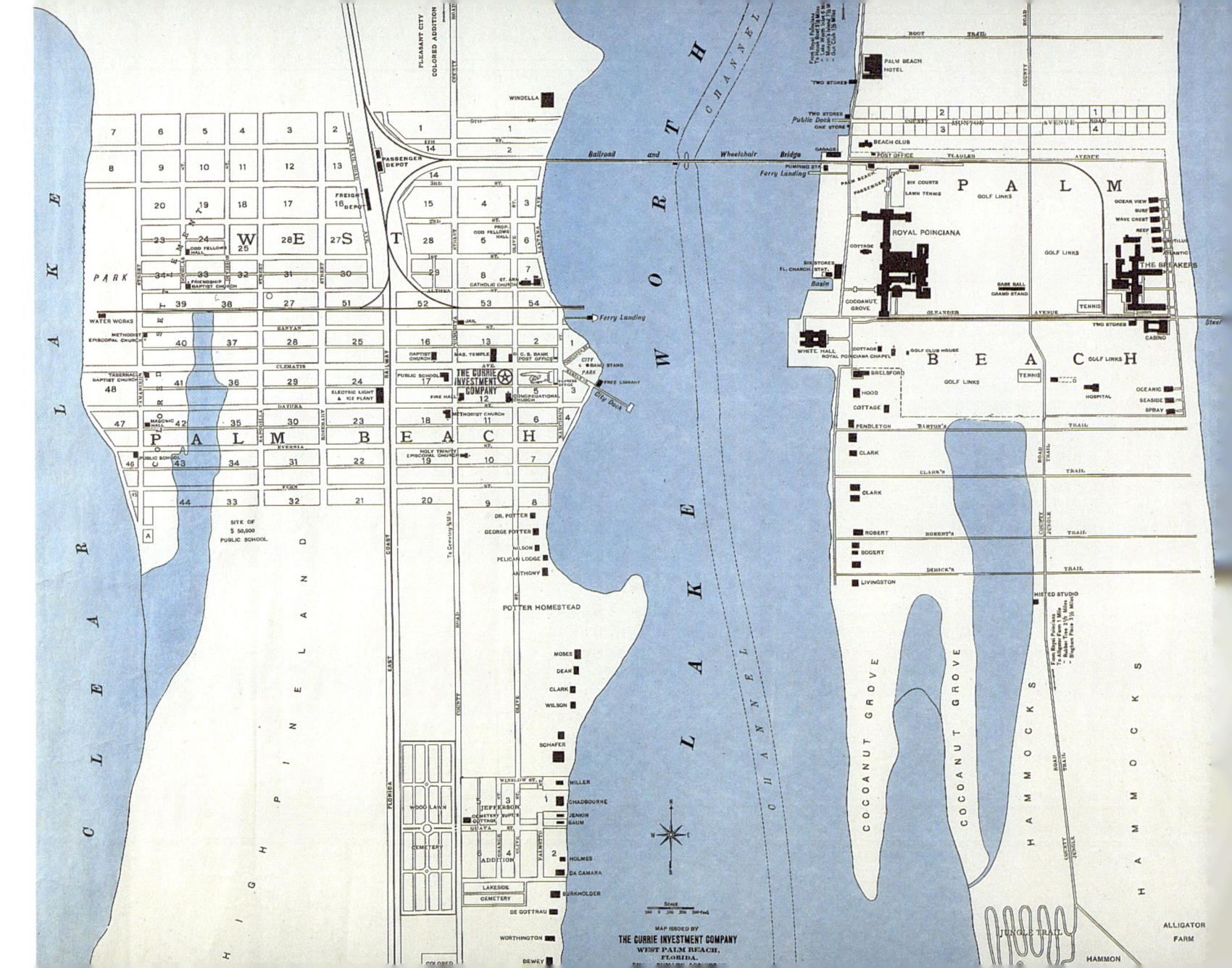

Photo courtesy of the Historical Society of Palm Beach County.